ARCHAE(
EXPLORE
EARLY AMERICA

BY STEPHANIE SIGUE

Editorial Offices: Glenview, Illinois • Parsippany, New Jersey • New York, New York

Sales Offices: Needham, Massachusetts • Duluth, Georgia • Glenview, Illinois
Coppell, Texas • Sacramento, California • Mesa, Arizona

When an **archaeologist** begins to study a group of people, he or she hopes to answer certain questions. When and where did these people live? What can we learn about how they lived? What kinds of things did they leave behind?

Scientists know that people lived in North America for many centuries before the arrival of Europeans. These American Indians, or Native Americans, inhabited each region of the continent, from the Atlantic coast to the Pacific coast and from the Great Lakes to the Gulf of Mexico. The varied natural resources of each region had a significant influence on how these groups lived. Our understanding of how American Indians lived long ago comes from the work of archaeologists as well as the knowledge passed on to American Indians today.

American Indians of the Eastern Woodlands

The name *Iroquois* refers to the members of several American Indian groups that include the Mohawk, the Seneca, the Onondaga, the Oneida, and the Cayuga. Each was a group living in the forested regions of the Eastern Woodlands.

Like many other American Indian groups, the Iroquois relied heavily on available natural resources. For example, they used wood from the abundant hardwood trees such as maple, elm, and ash to build their villages, homes, and some tools.

The Iroquois were farmers who usually constructed their villages on high ground so that they could more easily protect themselves against attacks. A tall fence of spiked logs served as a means of protection. The Iroquois also built lookouts from which villagers could watch for approaching enemies.

Within each village the Iroquois built longhouses. A **longhouse** had living space and places for storing things. Each was approximately 20 feet wide and between 75 to 120 feet long. The frame was constructed from wooden poles and covered with tree bark.

Many different families could live in a single longhouse, and if necessary, the dwelling could be extended to house more families. Each family had its own living space with dividers that separated them from other families and raised platforms for sleeping and storage. Cooking fires were placed in a center aisle.

This model shows an Iroquois longhouse.

This engraving shows a Creek log house and its inhabitants.

In what is the present-day Southeastern United States, American Indians lived in villages that had three common features. One feature was a circular meetinghouse with a domed room where the town leaders met. Another feature was a central town square, or stomp ground, for religious or political ceremonies. Still another feature was a large court on which ball games were played. Family homes were usually built around the village border.

The Creek, the Chickasaw, the Choctaw, and the Cherokee all lived in what is the present-day Southeastern United States. These groups built plain, rectangular dwellings. Their houses were wooden constructions and each dwelling had a sloped roof made from grasslike plants or straw.

Originally part of the Creek, the Seminole inhabited Florida where it was hot, humid, and swampy. Some Seminole lived in *chickees*. These small dwellings had thatched roofs and open sides and were built on platforms to avoid flooding during heavy rains. The Seminole hung cotton fabric from the beams of their homes to help keep out rain and insects.

The Seminole *chickee* had open sides and was built on a platform.

American Indians of the Great Plains

The Great Plains of the western and central United States were home to many different groups of American Indians. Some American Indian groups of the Great Plains lived in permanent villages and farmed, but moved from place to place during buffalo hunting season. Among these groups were the Pawnee, the Omaha, and the Osage, who lived in earth **lodges**.

These lodges were square with a floor built below ground level. Wooden poles were used for the walls and roof, which were covered with woven grass and a covering of earth. An opening, or smoke hole, was left in the roof's center.

The Mandan and Hidatsa lived in dome-shaped earth lodges.

Changing Ways of Life

In the 1500s Spanish explorers brought horses with them to North America. Their arrival changed the ways of life of American Indians of the Great Plains. Horses made hunting easier and allowed American Indian groups to travel farther and faster. Over time, many of these groups became nomads who moved from place to place.

The Mandan and the Hidatsa lived in villages along the upper Missouri River in North Dakota. They built earth lodges near the river and winter lodges closer to the forests, which supplied them with wood for fires.

Each earth lodge had a dome shape, was between forty and sixty feet wide, and about fifteen feet high. These lodges had a roof made of wooden rafters covered with willows, grass, and sod. Inside, animal hides separated the sleeping quarters from the rest of the living space. A family kept all of its belongings inside the home, including their dogs and horses. Horses were kept inside so they would not be stolen.

Most American Indian groups of the Great Plains were not sedentary, or stayed in one place. They were nomadic people who hunted buffalo and followed the herds that moved across the region. Because these people were always on the move, they needed lodging that was portable. Among the many nomadic groups who lived in the Great Plains were the Sioux, the Cheyenne, the Comanche, the Blackfoot, the Crow, and the Arapaho.

Tepees were covered with buffalo hides. Once a year each tepee was covered with a new, fresh hide.

The nomadic groups of the Great Plains designed a dwelling that could be taken down easily, packed up, carried away, and rebuilt. This was the **tepee**, with a cone-shaped frame made from long, tall wooden poles. The poles were tied together at the top. A tepee was covered with buffalo hides, which were replaced once a year.

Tepees started off small enough for trained dogs to help carry the poles and hides when a group moved. After groups of the Great Plains began to use horses, however, their tepees became larger. With horses they could move their tepees and other belongings more easily.

Wickiups

Other nomadic groups lived in homes that could be built quickly and then abandoned when they moved. The Paiute, the Shoshone, and the Ute groups lived in the Great Basin between the Sierra Nevada and Rocky Mountains. They built dwellings called wickiups, which had a cone shape and were made with a lightweight frame covered by thatched grass.

American Indians of the Desert Southwest

American Indians of the Desert Southwest built a variety of dwellings. The early Mogollon (moh-GOH-yohn) and the Hohokam (huh-HO-kum) people built pit houses that were partially underground. Each house was rectangular with wooden poles that leaned inward to support a roof. This method of building created inward-sloping walls. People covered the roof and walls with branches and grass topped with a thick layer of adobe mud.

Mesa Verde's largest cliff dwelling is called the Cliff Palace, and has 217 rooms and 23 kivas. A *kiva* is an underground room used for religious ceremonies.

American Indian cliff dwellings and **pueblos** are two of the most remarkable finds made by archaeologists in the Desert Southwest. Cliff dwellings were found in an area called Mesa Verde (MAY-seh VEHR-dee), which is located in the "Four Corners" region of the United States. This is where the present-day borders of Utah, Colorado, New Mexico, and Arizona meet. These amazing structures, built by an ancient group known as the Anasazi, are located below a **mesa** set among steep cliffs. Some of the buildings are small and housed only a few families. Others are much larger, apartment-like buildings that were inhabited by as many as 250 people.

Later the Anasazi left the Four Corners region, probably because of drought, building new communities farther south. The people who moved there built pueblos containing rooms stacked one on top of another. Each higher story is set back from the one below. A series of ladders made it possible for people to move among the dwellings.

Some huge pueblos, called great houses, have hundreds of rooms and underground chambers. Some of the largest and most famous examples are located in Chaco Canyon, New Mexico. One great house, Pueblo Bonito, has about eight hundred rooms. These structures were large enough to house as many as three thousand people, though archaeologists believe that fewer people actually lived there.

Art and Artifacts

Archaeologists are interested in more than just dwellings. They also look for **artifacts** such as tools, weapons, clothing, pottery, baskets, and decorative items—anything that can help them learn more about a culture.

Tools and weapons can tell scientists how people hunted for food. From the size and weight of a weapon, experts can tell how hunters used it.

People have found American Indian arrowheads all over the United States.

The beadwork on this Tlingit (TLING-git) ceremonial robe made in Alaska shows an eagle.

Before Europeans arrived in North America, American Indian women of the Eastern Woodlands made clothing from animal skins. They also decorated clothing with porcupine quills, which they often dyed before sewing onto a garment. When Europeans moved westward they brought new materials including glass beads with them. American Indian women began to use fancy beadwork to decorate their clothing.

A totem pole, such as this one, can be found in the Pacific Northwest.

Many American Indians were—and still are—expert potters, basket makers, carvers, and weavers. Scientists can date some of the American Indian pottery found by archaeologists back to prehistoric times. Much of the pottery is decorated with elaborate geometric designs. Archaeologists also have found many bowls decorated with animals such birds, frogs, and snakes.

The basketwork of the Chumash and the Pomo groups is especially detailed. These baskets are intricately woven and come in a variety of shapes and sizes. The workmanship is so skillful that the natural fibers are interwoven to create highly complicated designs.

The American Indians of the Pacific Northwest carved wooden **totem poles** to tell the story of a family tree. For example, a family might claim a relationship with a particular noble animal so that animal would be represented on the family's totem pole. Some totem poles are forty feet high.

Beautiful and colorful blankets woven by expert Navajo women are highly prized, especially large chiefs' blankets. These works of art contain intricate patterns that may combine stripes, zigzags, and diamond shapes. The Navajo today are also known for making silver jewelry inlaid with turquoise. They sometimes even create silver jewelry to decorate their horses.

Today many of the special objects made by American Indians are prized possessions of individuals and museums around the world. The National Museum of the American Indian, in Washington, D.C., contains more than 800,000 works of art. The pieces are from North and South America and span a period of ten thousand years. These artifacts, along with the knowledge passed on to American Indians today, have helped us to better understand how American Indians of long ago lived.

This Navajo blanket was made in the 1890s.

Glossary

archaeologist a scientist who studies the artifacts of people who lived long ago and draws conclusions from them

artifact an object made by people in the past

lodge a large, round hut built by American Indian groups of the Great Plains

longhouse a building used for shelter by the Iroquois

mesa a high, flat landform that rises steeply from the land around it

pueblo an American Indian village of the Desert Southwest region of the United States, typically made up of stone or adobe dwellings

tepee a dwelling built by American Indian groups of the Great Plains

totem pole a wooden post carved with animals or other images; often made by American Indians of the Pacific Northwest to honor ancestors or special events